Pandas

Kate Riggs

CREATIVE EDUCATION
CREATIVE PAPERBACKS

Published by Creative Education and Creative Paperbacks
P.O. Box 227, Mankato, Minnesota 56002
Creative Education and Creative Paperbacks are
imprints of The Creative Company
www.thecreativecompany.us

Design by Ellen Huber
Production by Chelsey Luther
Printed in the United States of America

Photographs by Corbis (DLILLC, Katherine Feng/
Minden Pictures, Jenny E. Ross, Keren Su), Dreamstime
(Isselee), Getty Images (Keren Su), National Geographic
Creative (MITSUAKI IWAGO/MINDEN PICTURES, JOE
PETERSBURGER), Shutterstock (Eric Isselee, lilavadee,
worldswildlifewonders), SuperStock (Minden Pictures)

Library of Congress Cataloging-in-Publication Data
Riggs, Kate.
Pandas / Kate Riggs.
p. cm. — (Seedlings)
Summary: A kindergarten-level introduction to pandas,
covering their growth process, behaviors, the forests they call
home, and such defining features as their black-and-white fur.
Includes index.
ISBN 978-1-60818-514-6 (hardcover)
ISBN 978-1-62832-114-2 (pbk)
1. Giant panda—Juvenile literature. 2. Adaptation (Biology)
—Juvenile literature. I. Title. II. Series: Seedlings.

QL737.C214R54 2015
599.789—dc23   2013051257

CCSS: RI.K.1, 2, 3, 4, 5, 6, 7;
RI.1.1, 2, 3, 4, 5, 6, 7; RF.K.1, 3; RF.1.1

9 8 7 6 5 4 3 2

TABLE OF CONTENTS

Hello, Pandas! 4

Life in China 6

Black-and-White Fur 8

Chewing Aids 11

Time to Eat! 12

Baby Pandas 14

What Do Pandas Do? 16

Goodbye, Pandas! 18

Picture a Panda 20

Words to Know 22

Read More 23

Websites 23

Index 24

Hello, pandas!

Pandas are small bears.

They live
in forests
in China.

Pandas have fur that is black and white.

They have claws on their paws.

Pandas have 42 teeth. Strong jaws help pandas chew tough food.

Pandas eat bamboo.
Bamboo is a grass
that looks like wood.

A baby panda is called a cub.

A cub leaves its mother when it is two. Adult pandas live alone.

Pandas climb trees.

They eat bamboo all day long. They fall asleep when they are tired.

Goodbye, pandas!

Picture a Panda

eye ....

mouth ....

leg ....

.... paw

fur

ear

nose

teeth

claws

China: a country in Asia, the biggest piece of land in the world

claws: curved, pointed nails on the paw

fur: the short, hairy coat of an animal

jaws: the upper and lower parts of the mouth

Read More

Olson, Bethany. *Baby Pandas*.
Minneapolis: Bellwether Media, 2014.

Schreiber, Anne. *Pandas*.
Washington, D.C.: National Geographic, 2010.

Websites

Panda Cam
http://zoo.sandiegozoo.org/cams/panda-cam
Watch the pandas at the San Diego Zoo.

Paper Bag Puppets Craft
http://www.enchantedlearning.com/crafts/puppets/paperbag/
Make puppets of a panda and other animals.

Index

bamboo **12, 17**

bears **6**

China **7**

claws **9**

climbing **16**

cubs **14, 15**

forests **7**

fur **8**

jaws **11**

sleeping **17**

teeth **11**